Supplement **American Red Cross Lifeguard Training**

ISBN 0-86536-145-2

Contents

Preface   v

CHAPTER 1:
Elementary Assists and Rescue Skills.   1
  Introduction.   2
  Reaching Assists.   2
  Wading Assists.   6
  Throwing Assists.   6
  Rescue Board and Surfboard.   10
  Rescue Tube.   12
  Rescue With Rescue Tube.   13
  Entering the Water   15
  Approach Strokes.   18
  The Ready Position.   18
  Rescue Kicks for Carrying a Victim.   19
  Surface Diving.   20

CHAPTER 2:
Mask, Fins, and Snorkel Skills.   23
  Introduction.   24
  Masks.   24
  Fins.   26
  Snorkels.   29
  Entering the Water Wearing Snorkeling Equipment   30
  Swimming Wearing Snorkeling Equipment.   31

CHAPTER 3:
Swimming Rescues.   33
  Submerged Victims.   34
  Surface Victims.   35
  Swimming Assists.   38
  Tows and Carries.   39
  Defense.   43
  Escapes.   44
  Multiple Near-Drowning Maneuver.   47
  Rescue Breathing in the Water   47

CHAPTER 4:
Spinal Injury Management   49
  Anatomy and Function of the Spine   50
  Principles for Handling
    a Victim of a Suspected Spinal Injury.   51
  General Rescue Procedures.   53
  Specific Rescue Techniques.   57
  Techniques for Stabilizing
    Suspected Spinal Injuries (Shallow Water).   58
  Techniques for Stabilizing
    Suspected Spinal Injuries (Deep Water).   68

Contents

CHAPTER 5:
Special Situations 71

Hypothermia 72

Heat Emergencies 75

Seizures 76

Preface

This supplement is designed to be used in conjunction with the
American Red Cross Lifeguard Training textbook, (Stock Number
321119, copyright 1983 and 1984) until the textbook is revised. It
covers fundamental skills previously taught in the Advanced
Lifesaving course. It also provides up-to-date technical information
on water rescue for spinal injuries and on the treatment of
hypothermia, seizures, and heat emergencies.

Chapters 1, 2, and 3 include information on assists and rescue
skills; rescue equipment; escapes; masks, fins, and snorkel skills;
and swimming rescues both with and without the aid of equipment.
Chapter 4 replaces the spinal injury section (pages 9-23 to 9-43) of
Chapter 9 in the *American Red Cross Lifeguard Training* textbook
(1983, 1984 edition). Chapter 5 replaces the section on epileptic
seizures and some of the section on hypothermia (pages 9-14 and 9-
15, 9-18 through 9-20) of Chapter 9 in the 1983, 1984 edition.

1

Elementary Assists and Rescue Skills

Introduction

Simple forms of assists, such as reaching, wading, and throwing, are the safest ways to help a person in difficulty without exposing the lifeguard to unnecessary dangers. When attempting to assist a victim, every rescuer, even a trained lifeguard, must maintain a position of safety. This position can be on shore, on a pier or pool deck, or from a small craft. The rescuer may also hold onto a rescue device such as a rescue tube. Since actual contact with a victim can be dangerous and is often unnecessary, the assist can usually be made by reaching, extending the reach, or using a boat. When it is necessary to actually swim to the victim, the lifeguard should stay out of reach whenever practical and extend some type of basic rescue equipment or a buoyant object to the victim.

Reaching Assists

In a reaching assist, you lie flat on the deck of the pool or on a pier, with the body anchored, and extend a hand to the victim. Grasp the victim's wrist from above *(Fig. 1)* and then slowly and carefully draw the victim to safety.

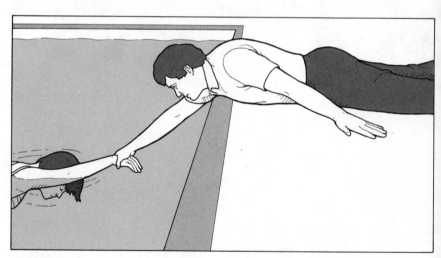

Figure 1
Reach From Deck

If you cannot reach the victim from the lying position, you can quickly slip into the water. While firmly hanging onto a support with one hand, reach out with your free hand and pull the victim to safety *(Fig. 2)*.

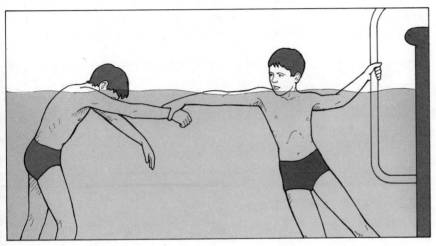

Figure 2
Arm Extension From Pool Ladder

If the victim is beyond arm's reach in the water, you may extend your legs to the victim while maintaining a firm grasp on a pool ladder, overflow trough, or piling *(Fig. 3)*. You may also extend a pole or a shepherd's crook.

While attempting a reaching assist, you should keep talking to the victim in an effort to calm and instruct the victim.

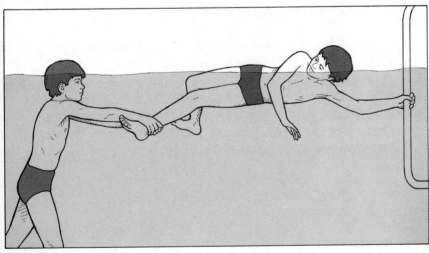

Figure 3
Leg Extension From Pool Ladder

Shepherd's Crook

The shepherd's crook is a long, light, aluminum pole with a blunted hook large enough to encircle a person's body. It is usually hung on a rack or on hooks at a convenient location. The hook end can be placed around the victim's chest under the armpits and is especially useful when a victim is unable to grasp an extended rescue device. Keep firmly braced and slowly pull the victim to safety *(Fig. 4)*.

Figure 4
Shepherd's Crook: Passive Victim

For active drowning victims, gently extend rounded hook end of shepherd's crook to the victim's chest, allowing the victim to grasp it, or extend the crook past the victim with the open side of the hook on the side opposite the victim. When the pole contacts the victim, turn it so that the open side encircles the victim's torso. While keeping your weight low and leaning away from the victim, pull the victim gently to safety *(Fig. 5)*.

Figure 5
Shepherd's Crook: Active Victim

Wading Assists

A lifeguard may advance into the water to about chest depth with comparative safety. Lean back toward shore before reaching out to grasp the victim *(Fig. 6)*. As with reaching assists, extending a pole or shepherd's crook is the preferred method of assisting the victim.

Figure 7
Free–Floating Support

Figure 6
Wading Assist

Figure 8
Maintaining Your Balance

Use of Free-Floating Support

You can avoid personal contact with the victim by using rescue equipment such as a kickboard, personal flotation device (PFD), buoyant cushion, or other similar buoyant object *(Fig. 7)*. The victim can then be encouraged to hang onto the object and kick or be pulled toward safety.

Throwing Assists

You can throw a ring buoy, throw bag, rescue tube, or other device so that the victim can grab it and be pulled to safety. In order to throw—
1. Get into a position that is safe and allows you to maintain your balance *(Fig. 8)*.
2. Bend your knees.

3. Step on the nonthrowing end of the rope *(Fig. 9)*.
4. Aim your throw so that the device will fall just beyond the victim but within reach *(Fig. 10)*.
5. When the victim has grabbed the device, keep talking reassuringly while slowly pulling the victim to safety, leaning your body weight away from the victim as you pull *(Fig. 11)*.

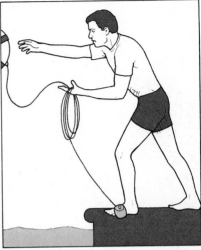

Figure 9
Step on the Nonthrowing End of the Rope

Figure 11
Pull Victim to Safety

Ring Buoy and Line

A ring buoy with line attached is available at many swimming areas and can be a valuable piece of rescue equipment for active victims. The ring buoy should weigh about two pounds and should be made of a buoyant material such as cork, kapok, foam rubber, or solid plastic. Fifty feet (approximately 15 meters) of 1/4-inch manila or polypropylene line should be attached to the ring. The other end of the line should have a wooden or plastic "lemon" to keep it afloat in case it gets thrown or pulled into the water and to keep it from slipping out from under your foot when you throw the buoy *(Fig. 12)*. The ring buoy should be hung where it will not be blown off its hook and should be positioned at a height where a rescuer can easily seize both it and the coil of line hung directly below it.

When grasping the ring buoy, your fingers should hold the underside of the ring buoy. The foot opposite the throwing hand is placed forward, across the end of the line in front of the "lemon." The coiled line hangs over the extended and open nonthrowing hand so that the line slides off over the fingertips.

Figure 10
Aim Throw Just Beyond Victim

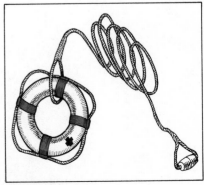

Figure 12
Ring Buoy With Line and "Lemon"

The throw is normally an underhand toss, with the buoy aimed just beyond the victim. After the victim has a firm grasp on the buoy or line, pull the victim to safety, being careful not to jerk the buoy out of the victim's grip.

In a wind, the throw should be upwind or upstream of the victim, not in a direct line to the victim, so that the drift will bring the buoy to the victim's reach. If the throw is inaccurate, pull the line in, coil it, and throw it out again.

If distance, inaccuracy, or the prevailing wind conditions keep the buoy out of reach of the victim, you must quickly decide what alternative exists. The safest alternative is to swim out with the buoy if no other conventional flotation rescue equipment is available. When you are within arm's reach of the victim, push the buoy to the victim *(Fig. 13)*. After the victim has a firm grasp on the buoy, tow him or her to safety by holding onto the buoy *(Fig. 14)* or by grasping the attached line well out of reach of the victim. Talking and giving instructions to the victim will usually help to keep the individual calm and under control during the tow to safety.

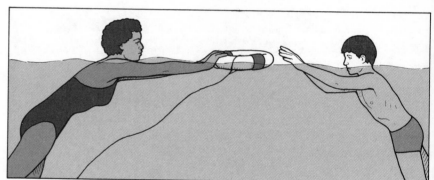

Figure 13
Ring Buoy: Push to Victim

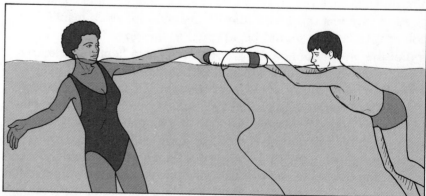

Figure 14
Ring Buoy: Tow to Safety

Heaving Line

A coiled length of line can be hung conveniently in place at swimming areas and makes an excellent rescue device for active victims *(Fig. 15)*. Before you throw the line, step on one end of it with your forward foot to secure it. Hang the coiled line over the open palm of the nonthrowing hand, and extend this hand forward at waist level. The coil should be split so that about half of the coil is in each hand. This gives the coil in the throwing hand sufficient weight so that it can be thrown with some accuracy.

Throw the coil with an underhand motion. Keep the palm of the nonthrowing hand open to allow the coil to run freely. The extended line should fall just beyond the victim and within reach of the victim's outstretched hands.

A heaving line can be thrown with better accuracy if it is weighted. The weight should be attached to the end that is thrown and preferably should be buoyant.

Figure 15
Heaving Line

Heaving Jug

A suitable piece of rescue equipment for home pools can be made from a gallon plastic jug containing about half an inch of water. Close and tape the top shut; then attach a length of line to the handle *(Fig. 16)*. The container and coil of line can then be hung conveniently in place at the swimming pool. Before throwing the equipment, secure the line by placing your forward foot on the line near the unattached end. Hang the coil of line over the open palm of the nonthrowing hand, and make the throw by grasping the handle of the jug and releasing it at the forward end of the swing. After the victim gets a firm grasp on the buoyant jug, he or she can be pulled in. Care should be taken to pull fast enough to keep the victim's head above water but smoothly enough so that the jug is not jerked from the victim's grasp.

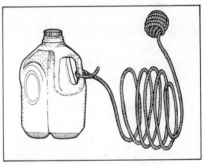

Figure 16
Heaving Jug

Throw Bag

A throw bag is a nylon bag containing from 50 to 75 feet of line that floats. A foam disk at the bottom of the bag gives the bag its shape and prevents it from sinking *(Fig. 17)*. For the initial throw, first ensure that the drawstring at the top of the bag is sufficiently loose to allow the line to slip out. Grasp the top of the bag in your throwing hand while holding the loop at the end of the line firmly with your other hand. Throw the bag with an underhand swing as with the heaving jug.

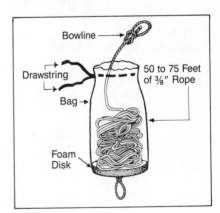

Bowline

Drawstring

50 to 75 Feet of ⅜" Rope

Bag

Foam Disk

Figure 17
Throw Bag

9

Figure 18
Approach the Victim

Figure 19
Grasp Victim's Wrist and
Slide off Board

Figure 20
Stroke or Paddle to Shore

Rescue Board and Surfboard

Modern boards are generally made of fiberglass and are of two types, rescue boards and surfboards. A rescue board is at least 10 feet long and about 22 inches wide and is buoyant enough to support the weight of two adults. A surfboard varies from 6 to 8 feet in length, is almost flat on the bottom, has at least one bottom fin, and usually has only enough buoyancy to support one person. It is adaptable for rescue, and it is useful in getting to a victim quickly and providing support for the victim in an emergency. The rescue board is preferred for rescue purposes because it can support two people.

The lifeguard should be thoroughly skilled in paddling and maneuvering the rescue board. Perfect your board handling and rescue skills in quiet water before attempting to use a rescue board in waves or rough water.

Launching the Board

The simplest method of launching is to place the board in the water at about knee depth and hold onto the sides about midway, pushing the board in front of you. While moving forward, get on the board, positioning your knees shoulder-width apart, and paddle in a kneeling position. For a more stable position, you can also lie on the board and paddle to a victim, but kneeling is generally more efficient for longer distances.

If you have enough strength and skill, a quicker launching method may be attempted. Hold the board vertically in front of you. Run into the water to knee depth, crouch, and drop the board somewhat forward and flat on the surface. Without losing momentum, quickly get onto the board in a kneeling position, knees shoulder-width apart, or lower your body to a lying-down position, and paddle out toward the victim.

Approaching the Victim

In quiet waters, simply point the board toward the victim and paddle, using either the crawl arm stroke or the butterfly arm stroke *(Fig. 18)*. Keep your head up and your eyes on the victim.

If you use proper timing, you can ride through moderate waves. When large waves are about to break on you, you should flatten out on the board, head down, and hold tight to the sides of the board.

Rescue of a Tired Victim Able to Get on the Board

When using a board to rescue a tired swimmer, approach the victim from the side while you paddle in a prone position. Grasp the victim's nearest hand or wrist and slide off the board on the side opposite the victim *(Fig. 19)*.

Help the victim extend his or her arms across the board and encourage the victim to relax and rest until calmed down. While the victim is resting, turn the board toward shore. Steady the board from the water. The victim then gets aboard by swimming onto the board while facing forward. When the victim is on the board lying flat on his or her stomach, get on the board from behind. You should lie down between the victim's legs. Your own legs may be off the board in the water and can be spread and used for additional stability. Adjust both your position and the victim's so that the front of the board is up high enough to clear the water slightly. Stroke or paddle the board to shore *(Fig. 20)*. The return to shore should be unhurried.

Rescue of a Panicky or Tired Victim Unable to Get on the Board

Approach the panicky or tired victim from the side. Grab the victim's wrist and slide off the board on the side opposite the victim, flipping the board over at the same time *(Fig. 21)*. The action of flipping the board will bring the victim partially onto the board. You will then be holding the victim's wrist across the board, with the board between you and the victim *(Fig. 22)*. At this point, calm the victim and explain how you are going to help and what the victim will have to do.

Place the victim's arms across the board. While holding the victim's arms with one hand, reach across the board and roll the board to right it *(Fig. 23)*. This will roll the victim's chest across and onto the board. You then rotate the victim so that the victim is lying in the middle of the board with his or her head toward the front *(Fig. 24)*. Next, swim onto the board behind the victim, adjust your and the victim's positions for proper balance, assume a prone paddling position, and start for shore *(Fig. 25)*.

Figure 21
Grab Wrist, Slide off Board, Flip Board

Figure 22
Board Between Rescuer and Victim

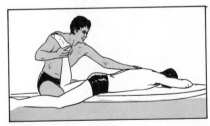

Figure 23
Roll Board to Right It

Figure 24
Position Victim

Figure 25
Paddle to Shore

☙ Rescue Tube

The rescue tube is a vinyl foam, free-floating support that can easily be towed to a victim. It has sufficient buoyancy to support one or more victims and is an indispensable piece of rescue equipment. It is flexible, can be wrapped around a victim or the lifeguard, and has no sharp or hard edges.

Use of Rescue Tube in a Throwing Assist

If a victim is struggling in the water close to safety, the ends of the rescue tube can be quickly clipped together, making an improvised ring buoy. Throw the tube with one hand and hold onto the webbing loop with the other *(Fig. 26)*, making a quick, simple rescue device. When the victim grasps the tube, you can easily and carefully pull the victim to safety.

Figure 26
Hold Webbing and Throw Rescue Tube

Rescue With Rescue Tube X

In most cases, the rescue tube is used without a trail line attached to shore. The lifeguard grasps the tube in one hand and loops the webbed shoulder strap over one shoulder and under the opposite arm *(Fig. 27)*. If entering from an elevation 3 feet high or less, you can make a "stride jump" *(Fig. 28)*. Let the tube go in midair, and as you hit the water, start stroking toward the victim. If entering from higher than 3 feet (for example, from a lifeguard chair), hold the rescue tube tight across your chest with your armpits hooked over its ends *(Fig. 29)*.

Figure 27
Loop Strap of Rescue Tube Over Shoulder

Figure 28
Stride Jump With Rescue Tube

Figure 29
Jump From Height With Rescue Tube

Figure 30
Run Into Water Carrying Rescue Tube

Figure 31
Extend Rescue Tube From Ready Position

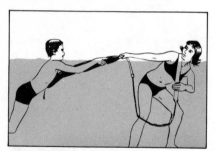

Figure 32
Hang Onto Strap and Tow Victim to Safety

Figure 33
Shallow Dive From Rocks With Rescue Tube

At a beach, make a "run and plunge" entry. Carrying the tube in one hand, run into the water, lifting your knees as high as possible with each stride in order to clear the water *(Fig. 30)*. At the point when running through deepening water becomes slower, make a shallow forward dive while letting go of the tube (the strap is over your shoulder) and swim toward the victim. Look up every few strokes to keep the victim in sight. Upon reaching a point within about 5 or 6 feet of the victim, stop and assume the ready position, and extend the tube to the victim *(Fig. 31)*. If the victim is excited or panicky, you may slip out of the shoulder loop to avoid being pulled close to the victim. After calming the victim, tow him or her to safety by hanging onto the strap at the end of the tube *(Fig. 32)*. Depending on the equipment and the help available, signal for help or signal for a trail line that can be connected to the tube so that you and the victim can be towed to shore.

If you have to enter from rocks and know the water depth but can't wade in, loop the rescue tube strap over one shoulder and hold the tube against your chest and stomach as you do a flat shallow dive *(Fig. 33)*. The tube keeps you high in the water. Then swim as usual to the victim.

A rescue buoy, pictured and described on page 7–5 of the *Lifeguard Training* textbook, can be used with the same entries as the rescue tube, with one exception. Do **not** use the rescue buoy when making a flat shallow dive to enter from or around rocks.

Rescue Tube Clasped Around Victim

The tube can be used even if you determine that the victim might not have sufficient strength to hang onto it. After reaching the victim, wrap the tube around the victim, clip the tube ends together, position the victim on his or her back, and tow to safety *(Fig. 34)*.

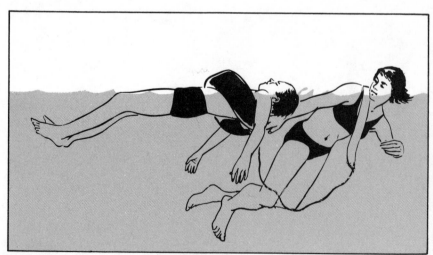

Figure 34
Rescue Tube Clasped Around Victim

Rescue Tube Clasped Around Lifeguard

Another method that can be used is to clip the tube around your upper body *(Fig. 35)*. Then approach, make contact, and tow the victim to shore using a cross-chest carry or armpit tow.

Rescue Tube With Trail Line Attached

When a victim is towed to shore using a rescue tube with a trail line attached, the victim seizes the tube and slides his or her head and chest about halfway up the tube, hanging onto the sides.

The lifeguard slides to the rear and straddles the victim, reaching under the victim's arms to get a handhold on the sides of the tube *(Fig. 36)*. When ready, the lifeguard signals to shore, and both lifeguard and victim are pulled to safety.

Figure 35
Rescue Tube Clasped Around Lifeguard

Entering the Water

The rescue of a distressed or near-drowning victim begins with an appropriate and safe entry by a lifeguard into the water. An entry may have to be made into a pool, wave pool, pond, river, lake, or the ocean. Depth of water, water clarity, knowledge of bottom conditions, height above water, distance to the victim, and stress level of the victim are all factors that help determine the type of entry employed by a lifeguard. Depending on the factors present, you may use one of the following entries to enter the water during a rescue attempt:

- **Stride Jump:** The purpose of the stride jump is to permit you to jump safely into water at least 5 feet deep, while keeping the victim in sight. This entry is appropriate from poolsides or docks 3 feet in height or less. The entry is made by leaping into the water with the legs held in a stride or scissors kick position, while leaning the body forward at an angle of approximately 45 degrees *(Fig. 37)*. The hands and arms can be fully extended behind or to the side of the body or crossed in front of the chest. Upon entry, squeeze or scissors the legs together to provide upward thrust. If the arms are extended behind the body or to the side, the hands should be pulled forward and down upon entry. If the arms are crossed in front of the chest, the hands should press down and move outward in breaststroke fashion.

Figure 36
Victim and Lifeguard Towed by Trail Line

Figure 37
Stride Jump

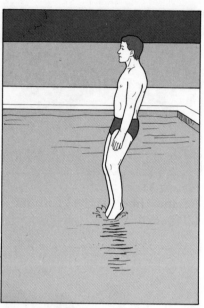

Figure 38
Feetfirst Entry

- **Feetfirst Entry From a Height:** A feetfirst entry should be used when you must enter the water from a height of more than 3 feet. Do not attempt this entry if the water depth is unknown. A feetfirst entry should be made by entering the water in a vertical position with arms at your sides, legs together and knees slightly flexed, head erect, and eyes on the victim *(Fig. 38)*. When your head goes under water, extend your arms outward while you spread your legs in a scissors or breaststroke position. Once descent has ceased, swim to the surface.

  This entry can also be accomplished using the rescue tube. Loop the strap over your shoulder, hold it tightly across your chest, and hook your armpits over the ends.

- **Ease In:** This entry from poolside or from a dock must be used to rescue a victim with a suspected spinal cord injury or when water depth is less than 5 feet or is unknown. Splash and ripple action of the water should be kept at a minimum when you are rescuing the victim of a spinal injury. Enter by sitting down on the edge of the pool or dock, facing the water. Keeping your eyes on the victim, gently slide into the water *(Fig. 39)*.

- **Beach:** Beach lifeguards often enter the water running. When entering and running in shallow water, lift your legs up high to avoid tripping *(Fig. 40)*. As water deepens to the point where running is no longer possible, lean forward while springing off one foot and do a shallow dive. Be careful when using this entry to keep your body, arms, and head in the streamlined position. Dropping either head or arms could result in changing the body's angle of entry from shallow to deep. Such an entry could cause your head to hit the bottom. A flat entry also enables you to begin swimming immediately.

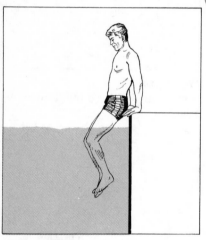

Figure 39
Ease–In Entry

Figure 40
Beach Entry

Shallow Dive: Lifeguards standing on a dock or at poolside often have the opportunity to begin a rescue by using a variation of a competitive racing dive. This shallow dive provides a quick start, keeping you near the surface of the water and enabling you to begin swimming immediately.

To perform a shallow dive, step to dock or pool edge, spread your feet slightly, and place your toes over the edge to help prevent slipping. Crouch down, bending your knees enough to make your back parallel to the water's surface. Lean forward, swing your arms back, and prepare to spring forward. Press against the dock or pool edge with your toes, extend your legs, and swing your arms forward until fully extended over your head *(Fig. 41)*. Do not pike or elevate your hips. Drop your head slightly, allowing your hands to enter first. While this dive provides a shallow angle, it should be used only where water and bottom conditions are known, and the water depth is at least 5 feet.

Figure 41
Shallow Dive

Approach Strokes

Speed is an essential component of every rescue. An active drowning victim is not usually on the surface for more than 60 seconds. The lifeguard should therefore use the fastest strokes available and make occasional visual contact. The best approach strokes are the crawl and the breaststroke.

- **Crawl Stroke:** The crawl is without question the fastest of all strokes. As an approach stroke, it should be performed with the face in the water to lessen frontal resistance and maximize speed. While swimming toward the victim, you should lift your head occasionally while breathing and refocus on the victim.
- **Breaststroke:** While the breaststroke is slower than the crawl, it is a very effective approach stroke that allows the lifeguard to swim on the surface or underwater. The breaststroke also provides other advantages, combining speed and energy conservation with the opportunity for a quick look, since breathing is done while looking straight ahead. It is useful in rough water.

Note: It is important in making a rescue that the lifeguard remember to conserve enough energy for the return trip.

The Ready Position

In preparation for making contact with a victim, you should assume the "ready position." This position prepares you to defend yourself and swim away if the victim tries to grab you while you are making a rescue. You should stop approximately 6 feet from the victim, determine what rescue technique the situation requires, attempt to reassure the victim, and assume the ready position.

To get into the ready position, stop beyond the victim's reach (approximately 6 feet), tuck your legs under your body, and sweep your arms forward beneath the surface while leaning on your side and away from the victim. Then use a sculling action to move toward the victim for contact. The ready position places you in a good swimming position before contact has been made during a rescue.

Rescue Kicks for Carrying a Victim

- **Inverted Scissors Kick:** This kick is done like the normal scissors kick except the leg nearer to the surface (top leg) extends back and the leg farther from the surface (bottom leg) extends forward *(Fig. 42)*.

Figure 42
Inverted Scissors Kick

- **Elementary Backstroke Kick:** A lifeguard may possess a stronger elementary backstroke kick than scissors kick and may choose to use this kick *(Fig. 43)*.

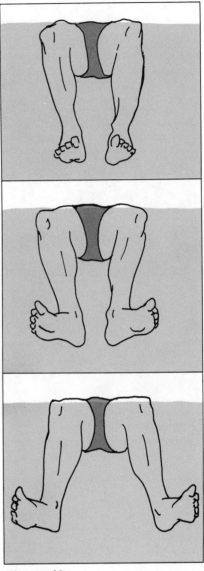

Figure 43
Elementary Backstroke Kick

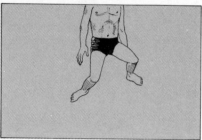

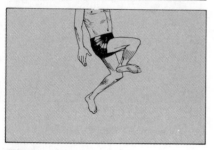

Figure 44
Rotary Kick

- **Rotary Kick:** This kick, developed for use in water polo, also has applications in water rescue. The kick uses an alternating breaststroke movement where each leg kicks through a breaststroke range of motion *(Fig. 44)*. Applications for this kick include the ready position and carrying a victim.

Surface Diving

Surface diving is a skill that enables a lifeguard to submerge from the surface of the water to moderate depths during rescue or search for a submerged victim. Three surface dives are useful.

- **Feetfirst Surface Dive:** This dive is the safest to use in murky water or in water of unknown depth. Begin the dive while treading water. Press downward vigorously with your hands and simultaneously execute a strong scissors or breaststroke kick. At the conclusion of the thrust of the hands and legs, the body is raised high in the water. Allow your body to sink, hands by your sides, while in this position until your head is submerged and downward momentum begins to slow. Rotate your wrists, turning palms outward, and press vigorously upward (toward the surface) with your hands *(Fig. 45)*. Recover the arms to the side and pull again, if desired, or level out and swim forward underwater.

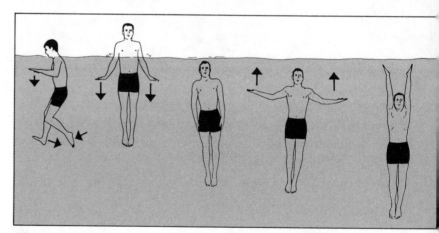

Figure 45
Feetfirst Surface Dive

- **Pike or Tuck Surface Dive:** In clear water, swim the breaststroke on the surface until ready to dive. Then lower your head, flex at the hips while pressing your arms and palms backward to the thighs. Lift and extend the legs while recovering the arms forward in line with the body. Open your eyes and look down while lifting your legs *(Fig. 46)*. When all movements are done properly, your legs will rise above the surface, bent at the knees for tuck and straight at the knees for pike, to aid you in making a rapid descent.

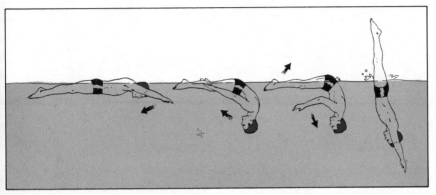

Figure 46
Pike Surface Dive

- **Quick Surface Dive:** The quick surface dive is almost identical to the pike surface dive and is used when speed is important, such as in the event an exhausted victim slips beneath the surface during your approach. The dive starts with good forward momentum, achieved by using the crawl stroke. To execute the dive, take a breath and plunge your lead arm downward and then bring the other arm down to meet the extended arm while flexing at the hips *(Fig. 47)*. Lift your legs high up in the air so that the weight of the legs aids in descending. Open your eyes and look down while lifting your legs.

Figure 47
Quick Surface Dive

Mask, Fins, and Snorkel Skills

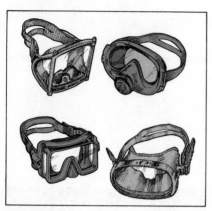

Figure 48
Types of Masks

Introduction

Masks, fins, and snorkels are equipment used for swimming enjoyment and underwater exploration. This equipment is also used by lifeguards for pool maintenance, underwater search and recovery, and keeping a victim with a spinal cord injury afloat in deep water. Quick rescue of submerged victims may depend on ready accessibility and proficient use of masks, fins, and snorkels. They should be provided to lifeguards at aquatic facilities, and practice with them should be incorporated into all in-service training programs.

Masks

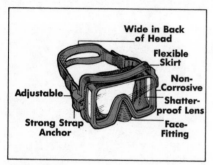

Figure 49
Parts of Mask

Characteristics of Masks

A mask should be made of soft, flexible rubber or silicone *(Fig. 48)*. It should have untinted, tempered safety glass, a noncorrosive metal or plastic band, and a strap that is easily adjusted *(Fig. 49)*. Some masks have a molded nose, making it possible for the person wearing the mask to pinch his or her nose in order to equalize pressure in the ears upon descent. Some masks have a one-way purge valve that allows the swimmer to clear water from the mask without removing the mask.

Defogging the Faceplate

To prevent condensation from forming on the inside of the faceplate, rub saliva or a commercially produced defogging solution on the inside of the glass. Then rinse the mask with water.

Proper Mask Fitting

To determine if a mask fits properly, place the mask against your face without using the strap, making sure your hair is out of the way *(Fig. 50)*. Inhale through your nose. If the mask remains in place without being held, it is airtight. Adjust the strap to hold it in place. Next, put your face in the water with the mask on. If it leaks, tighten the strap.

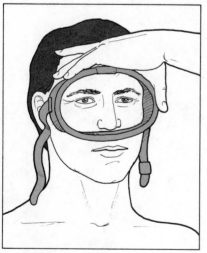

Figure 50
Test Mask for Fit

Clearing a Mask of Water

Even if your mask fits properly, small amounts of water may leak in while you are swimming underwater. Practicing clearing the mask in shallow water will increase your confidence in using the mask.

Fit the mask to your face as described in the previous section. Submerge in a sitting position and tilt or lift the mask away from your face, slowly allowing water to enter. Surface and stand up, taking a breath through your mouth. Tilt your head back slightly. Place two or three fingers (or palm of one hand) on the top of the faceplate and press in against your forehead *(Fig. 51)*. At the same time, exhale forcefully through your nose. This forces the water out at the lower edge of the mask *(Fig. 52)*. Repeat as often as necessary until you are comfortable with this step. Continue practicing underwater in shallow water.

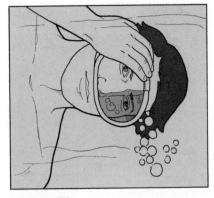

Figure 53
Clear Mask: Horizontal

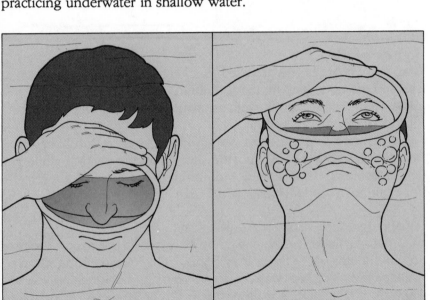

Figures 51 and 52
Press Faceplate Against Forehead and Force Water Out

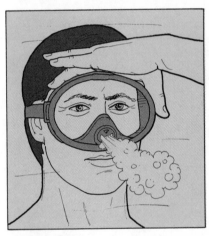

Figure 54
Clear Mask: Purge Valve

In deep water, the mask may be cleared while you are swimming in a horizontal position. This is accomplished by turning the head to either side, placing two or three fingers or the palm of one hand on what was the side, but is now the top, of the mask. Press firmly, exhale through your nose, and water will be forced out through the lower side *(Fig. 53)*.

If the mask has a purge valve, blow forcefully through your nose, and the water will be forced out the one-way valve *(Fig. 54)*.

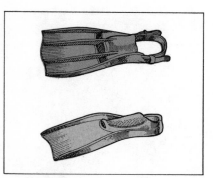

Figure 55
Types of Fins

Relieving Mask and Ear Pressure

When a diver descends, the surrounding water causes an increase in pressure forcing the mask onto the diver's face and causing discomfort, pain, and possible injury. To help relieve this pressure, exhale a small amount of air from your nose into the mask.

Ear pressure may be relieved by placing your thumbs along the bottom of the mask, pressing it against your nostrils, and attempting to exhale. If the mask is equipped with a molded nose, use it to pinch your nostrils while attempting to exhale. Repeated attempts may have to be made before pressure in your ears is relieved. Some people can clear their ears by swallowing. Do not attempt to go deeper until you are successful in clearing your ears.

Fins

Types of Fins

Two basic types of fins are used in diving: the full-foot or shoe fin, and the open-heel fin that is held in place with a heel strap *(Fig. 55)*. Fins should fit well, as chafing can occur with fins that fit incorrectly or too tightly.

Open-heel fins are often worn with socks or with rubber or nylon boots. Such boots provide warmth and protection while you are swimming. They also provide protection when fins are removed for walking in shallow water or on land.

Walking With Fins

Wet your fins and feet before putting fins on, as this makes it easier to pull the fins over your feet or boots. While wearing fins, always walk sideways or backward to avoid tripping. Look behind you to keep from falling while walking backward on land.

Kicking With Fins

The most common kick with fins is the modified flutter kick. You can use it when you are faceup, facedown, or on your side. The kicking action is deeper and slower and has a greater knee bend than the flutter kick *(Fig. 56)*. While swimming on the surface, be sure to keep the fins under water to maximize propulsion. Since they make treading water easier, fins are very helpful in deep water rescues.

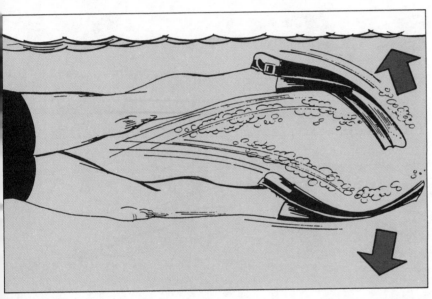

Figure 56
Fins: Modified Flutter Kick

A dolphin kick can also be used for surface and underwater swimming. Keep your legs together. Bend your knees to bring the fins up and arch your back. Then straighten your legs and bend forward at the waist to bring the legs down *(Fig. 57)*. Bend your knees again to bring the fins up, straighten your body, and arch your back.

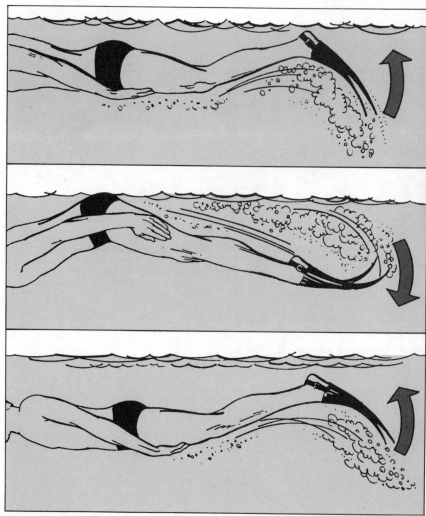

Figure 57
Fins: Dolphin Kick

Snorkels

Characteristics of Snorkels

Snorkels are rubber or silicone tubes that enable you to swim facedown on the surface and breathe without turning or moving your head. They can be "J" or "L" shaped, or shaped like a flexible "I," with straight or flared tops *(Fig. 58)* and should have a soft mouthpiece. Snorkels should be 12 to 15 inches in length and at least 3/4-inch in diameter. The bigger the inner diameter, the easier it is to breathe, but the harder it is to clear the snorkel.

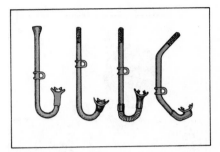

Figure 58
Types of Snorkels

The top of the snorkel barrel should have a fluorescent safety band around it so that a swimmer can be easily seen. The snorkel is attached to the mask strap with a snorkel keeper, a small piece of rubber or plastic.

Using the Snorkel

After attaching the snorkel to your mask, place the mask on your face and the snorkel in your mouth. The mouthpiece should fit between your teeth and lips *(Fig. 59)*. Adjust the position of the snorkel in the keeper and on the mask strap for a comfortable fit. The snorkel should rest by your ear when your face is in the water.

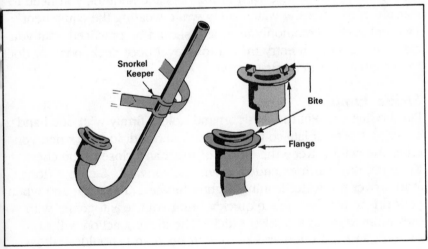

Figure 59
Parts of Snorkel

When using the snorkel, put the mouthpiece completely in your mouth with the teeth guards between your teeth and lips. Seal the snorkel by holding your lips tightly around the barrel. Practice breathing with your face out of the water until you feel comfortable.

While standing in chest-deep water, put your face in the water and practice breathing. After becoming comfortable with this skill, practice snorkel breathing while swimming on the surface with your face in the water.

Figure 60
Clear Snorkel by Exhaling

Figure 61
Clear Snorkel by Tilt Method

Figure 62
Stride Jump

Clearing the Snorkel

You need to know how to clear water out of the snorkel because it will fill up when you dive (and sometimes while you are swimming on the surface). Practice flooding and clearing the snorkel in shallow water. Take a breath and submerge deep enough to flood the snorkel. Return to the surface, keep your face in the water, and exhale forcefully through the snorkel. A forceful exhalation will expel the water from the tube *(Fig. 60)*. Then inhale carefully and slowly in case a small amount of water remains in the snorkel. Exhale again to force out any remaining water and then continue to breathe normally.

Another way to empty the snorkel is by the tilt method *(Fig. 61)*. As you surface, tilt your head back, angle the snorkel down, look up, and exhale gently. When your snorkel clears the surface, return your head to a facedown position and inhale gently. If there is still water in the snorkel, blow forcefully.

Entering the Water Wearing Snorkeling Equipment

After gaining confidence with mask, fins, and snorkel, you need to learn how to enter the water safely while wearing the equipment. Two entries are commonly used and should be practiced until you can make a smooth entry from a low-level pool deck, boat, or dock. Never attempt a head-first entry!

Stride Jump

Put the fins on. Put the mask on and hold it firmly with one hand covering the faceplate so that the mask is not dislodged when you enter the water. Keep the elbow of that hand close to the chest. Keep the other arm extended down and forward. Step out (long stride) over the water leaning slightly forward *(Fig. 62)*, and when your fins touch the surface quickly bring your legs together with your toes pointed, as in the scissor kick. The kicking action will stop the downward motion and keep your head and shoulders above the water.

Sit-In

This entry can be begun from a standing or sitting position with your back to the water. Pull the fins on. Pull the mask on. Hold it firmly with one hand covering the faceplate and your elbow close to your chest. Place your other hand by your side. If standing, place your heels even with the edge of the pool. Tuck your chin on your chest, pike at the hips, and sit into the water keeping your legs straight. If entering from a boat, sit on the side and hold on with one hand while holding on to the mask with your other hand. Tuck your chin on your chest and lean back into the water *(Fig. 63)*.

This entry may leave you somewhat disoriented, and it affords no protection against objects in the water. Do not use this entry if you are more than 2 feet above the water or in water less than 8 feet deep.

Figure 63
Sit–In Entry

Swimming Wearing Snorkeling Equipment

The normal swimming position when you are wearing mask, fins, and snorkel is horizontal with your arms at your side and your face in the water *(Fig. 64)*. When using a snorkel, you can scan the bottom for a submerged victim or object without having to lift your face to breathe.

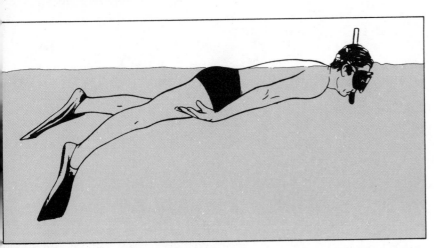

Figure 64
Swim With Snorkeling Equipment

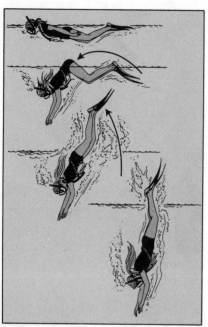

Figure 65
Surface Dive With Snorkel

Surface Diving and Resurfacing

You perform a surface dive by rolling forward into a tuck or pike position to descend *(Fig. 65)*. Upon returning to the surface, sto look up, listen, and extend a hand overhead before surfacing. This safety precaution should be standard procedure when surfacing. Upon reaching the surface, clear your snorkel and resume normal breathing.

Swimming Underwater

The easiest way to swim underwater while wearing fins is to use you legs only. Your arms can be carried forward for protection when swimming in unclear water.

Submerged Victims

When a victim has disappeared beneath the surface, recovery must be made with the utmost speed if the victim is to be resuscitated. The location of the victim must be reasonably well established. Note that observations of untrained eyewitnesses are often inaccurate in their estimation of time, location, and circumstances surrounding a drowning.

While use of scuba equipment is the preferred method of underwater search and recovery in deep open-water accidents, a scuba rescue team is usually not immediately available. Therefore, lifeguards should be able to use less effective but immediate means of searching for and recovering a submerged victim. During such a rescue, the facility's emergency action plan should be activated and a scuba rescue team summoned.

Depth of water, clarity, temperature, waves, and current are all factors that must be considered in search and rescue. The availability of additional help and search and rescue equipment will determine the best procedures to use.

Recovery of a Submerged Victim by Surface Diving

If the victim goes under as you are approaching, you must get to the victim immediately. Keep your eyes fixed on the spot where the victim was last seen. Upon reaching that spot, perform a surface dive *(Fig. 66)*. When you locate the victim, grasp the victim's wrist, arm, or armpit from behind. Plant your feet if the bottom is firm,

Figure 66
Locating Submerged Victim

push off, and stroke and kick your way to the surface. If the bottom is soft or muddy, you must depend entirely on your arm and leg strokes to bring the victim to the surface. Begin rescue breathing as soon as possible after you reach the surface.

When there is doubt as to the location of a victim, you must survey the situation and plan a course of action. Determine the general area in which the victim is supposed to have gone under. Look for bubbles rising to the surface. If there are none and the water is clear, systematically swim across the area with your face in the water and scan the bottom. If the bottom is dark, light clothing, a bright swimming suit, or the gleam of bare arms and legs may be detected.

On white sand, dark clothing and dark hair can indicate the location of a victim. When the victim is located, surface dive, swim to a position behind him or her, grasp the wrist, upper arm, or armpit, and swim to the surface. Begin rescue breathing on the surface, if possible.

In murky or dark water where the bottom can be reached by surface diving, the area in which the swimmer was last seen should be searched by using a series of systematic feetfirst surface dives. Attempt to cover the designated area of the bottom in a series of overlapping lanes until the victim is found or until you are satisfied that the victim is not in that section. After each dive, swim along the bottom for two or three body lengths and then surface. Move back about 3 feet and then repeat the process. Attempting to swim along the bottom for a considerable distance can be exhausting; and, if the victim is not found on the first few attempts, you may be unable to continue long enough to cover a designated area in the search. Repeated dives even in shallow water (8 to 10 feet) are physically very demanding. Using a systematic formation or pattern whereby every square foot of the bottom can be examined is the best technique, whether the searching is done by a single guard or a group of lifeguards.

Surface Victims

The approach to a drowning victim must be made with great speed and care. You need to determine if the victim is active or passive, and then select an appropriate approach. Upon contact, if the victim is not breathing, you must decide whether to begin rescue breathing or tow the victim. The decision to begin rescue breathing or towing will depend on the victim's physical condition, environmental factors (waves, water temperature), your physical condition, and how close you are to safety. The proper tow or carry should be selected quickly.

Swim or Dive to the Rear

An active victim can be rescued by diving and swimming underwate[r]
to the rear of the victim, or by swimming on the surface around an[d]
behind the victim. When using a surface approach, you should
perform an appropriate entry and swim quickly to a position
immediately behind the victim *(Fig. 67)*. Assume a ready position[,]
scull closer to the victim, and grasp the armpit to level the victim.
Apply a cross-chest carry and take the victim to the closest point o[f]
safety. If the return distance with the victim is greater than 40 feet,
use a single or double armpit tow.

Figure 67
Swim or Dive Behind Victim

Front Surface Approach

If a victim is facedown at or near the surface of the water, a front surface approach should be used. Enter and swim quickly to within 6 feet of the victim. Stop and assume the ready position. In the ready position, scull to the victim and grasp the underside of the victim's wrist (your right hand on the victim's right wrist or left hand to left wrist). Begin kicking for momentum and pull the victim's arm toward you while rotating the victim's wrist, turning it palm up. The pull and turn will roll the victim over onto his or her back. *(Fig. 68)* Continue to safety using the wrist tow, any other appropriate tow, or the cross-chest carry.

Figure 69
Rear Approach: Assume Ready Position

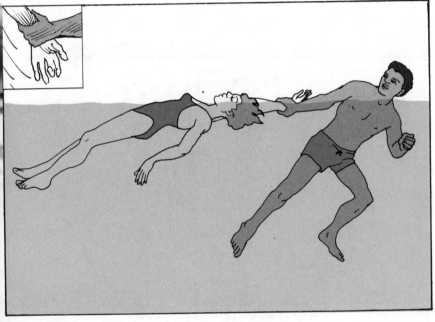

Figure 68
Grasp Underside of Wrist; Roll Victim Onto Back

Figure 70
Grasp Victim's Armpit

Rear Approach

This approach is used when the victim is on the surface (active or passive) or near the surface (passive). Enter the water and quickly approach to within 6 feet of the victim. Assume the ready position *(Fig. 69)*. If the victim is passive **or** the return distance with an active victim is greater than 40 feet, use a single or double armpit tow or rescue equipment. If the victim is active and the return distance is less than 40 feet, move closer by sculling and use an armpit tow to level the victim, then apply a cross-chest carry. If not using equipment, you should approach, assume the ready position, scull closer to the victim, and grasp the victim's armpit (right hand to right armpit or left to left) *(Fig. 70)*. Tow the victim by swimming sidestroke or using the elementary backstroke kick. You may choose a single armpit tow or a cross-chest carry to take the victim to safety. If possible, keep talking to reassure the victim.

Swimming Assists

A swimming assist may be used to help a distressed swimmer. An assist often involves a carry or a tow.

Assist on Front or Back

Enter the water and swim quickly to the person needing assistance. Swim alongside and grasp the victim by the upper arm near the armpit (thumb up) to support the victim and keep his or her head above water *(Fig. 71)*. Keep talking reassuringly, and swim next to the victim using a modified sidestroke or breaststroke. Maintain a firm grip on the victim while swimming to safety.

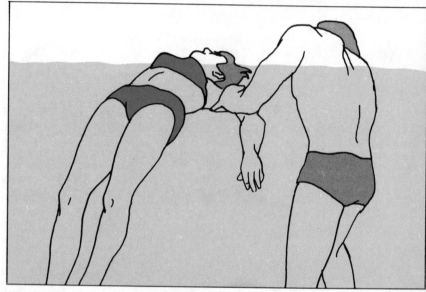

Figure 71
Assist on Front or Back

Assist by Two Lifeguards

Two lifeguards may be needed to assist a very large or nonbuoyant victim. The lifeguards should be positioned along each side of the victim, grasping firmly each upper arm with thumbs up *(Fig. 72)*. Using a modified sidestroke or breaststroke, they assist the victim to safety, reassuring the victim as they go.

Figure 72
Assist by Two Lifeguards

Tows and Carries

The purpose of a tow or a carry is to transport a victim to safety and/or to a place where additional emergency assistance can be provided if needed. A tow or a carry must be accomplished quickly and with concern for the victim's ability to breathe. Carrying and towing techniques must not inhibit the victim's breathing. Remember that whatever carry or tow you are using, you should tell the victim to relax and talk reassuringly to him or her.

Recognize that tows and carries require you to be in good physical condition because the size of the victim, the water temperature, waves, currents, and distance to safety can combine to create difficult rescue conditions. You must be aware of your strengths and weaknesses in relation to the victim and environment in making a swimming rescue.

Figure 74
Grasp the Victim's Armpits

Figure 75
Kick to Become Horizontal in Water

Single Armpit Tow

This tow may be used for either active or passive victims and is well suited for use with a rear approach. After you assume the ready position, use your hand that is closer to the victim to grasp the victim's armpit (right hand to the right armpit, or left to left). Place your fingers under the arm and into the armpit with your thumb in the up position along the outside of the victim's arm *(Fig. 73)*. Rest your head on the water and begin swimming the elementary backstroke or sidestroke. You can use either a regular or inverted scissors kick.

Figure 73
Single Armpit Tow

Double Armpit Tow

The double armpit tow is used with a rear approach for either an active or passive victim. This tow is usually selected by lifeguards who prefer the breaststroke kick over the scissors kick, although a scissors or rotary kick can be used. Prior to contact with the victim, assume a ready position and grasp the victim's armpits simultaneously with fingers under the arms and thumbs up *(Fig. 74)*. A rotary kick may be useful at this point until you and the victim are both horizontal on your backs, with your legs and lower body beneath the victim *(Fig. 75)*. Keep the victim's head back. Reassure the victim that all is well. If more control is needed, you can slide both your hands under the armpits, across the victim's chest, and hold on to one of your wrists with your opposite hand.

When choosing the elementary backstroke kick, assume a modified ready position by maintaining a vertical body position. Do not turn on your side. Reach in and grasp both the victim's armpits simultaneously, lay your head back, and begin kicking with short, powerful thrusts of the legs.

Wrist Tow

The wrist tow is only used for a passive victim and is a logical carry to use when making a front surface approach. Turn the victim over onto his or her back by grabbing the underside of the victim's wrist, with right hand to right wrist or left hand to left wrist *(Fig. 76)*. Then lean backward, pulling the victim's arm across your body, twisting the wrist in line with the pull. Swim sidestroke or elementary backstroke, maintaining a fully extended towing arm. A strong sidestroke is required to maintain the momentum necessary to keep the victim's face above water.

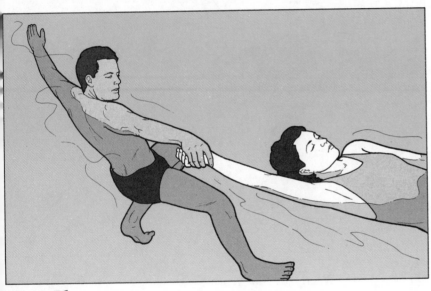

Figure 76
Wrist Tow

Figure 78
Cross–Chest Carry

Changing From Wrist Tow to Armpit Tow

Choppy water conditions may require a change to a single or double armpit tow. To change from a wrist tow to an armpit tow, continue to kick vigorously to maintain forward momentum. As you pull the victim toward you with your hand on the victim's wrist, use your free hand to grasp the victim's opposite armpit *(Fig. 77)*. Release the victim's wrist and continue with the single armpit tow. You should maintain contact with the victim while changing positions.

Figure 77
Change From Wrist Tow to Armpit Tow

Cross-Chest Carry

The cross-chest carry is used primarily for an active victim. It is designed specifically for the comfort of the victim and is difficult to use for long distances even by well-conditioned lifeguards. When performed correctly, it allows the victim to sit up or elevate the head and shoulders above water. Once he or she is able to breathe, the victim will usually stop struggling and relax. However, the victim's elevated body tends to force the lifeguard's head under water, making it difficult to get consecutive breaths.

The cross-chest carry can be used after a rear approach. Assume the ready position after swimming to within 6 feet of the victim and scull in before making contact. Grasp the victim at the armpit and begin kicking and pulling vigorously to move the victim from a vertical to a horizontal position. While in this position, reach under the victim's arm (right arm to right side, left arm to left side) with your free hand and cross the victim's lower chest until your hand is holding on to the victim's opposite side *(Fig. 78)*. Once in this position, let go at the armpit and kick vigorously to maintain momentum during the carry. Once the carry is under way, you may slide your arm up or down the victim's body depending on how high the victim lifts his or her head above the water.

Alternate Cross-Chest Carry

In the alternate cross-chest carry, after leveling the victim and getting underway, bring your free arm over the corresponding shoulder of the victim, across the chest, until your hand is in contact with the victim's side, just below the armpit *(Fig. 79)*.

Hold the victim in a firm, snug grip against the side of your chest. This strong, steady hold will instill a sense of security in the victim. You will be on your side, and your hip will be directly beneath the small of the victim's back. Use the sidestroke with either the regular or inverted scissors kick. Check to see that the victim's face is clear of the water. This carry does not allow the victim to be as clear of the water as the cross-chest carry does.

Figure 79
Alternate Cross–Chest Carry

Defense

In unusual circumstances, you may be confronted face-to-face with a panicky victim. Recommended approaches have been purposely designed to prevent this by having the lifeguard approach the active victim from behind. If you approach from the front, the victim may attempt to grab your head, shoulder, or arm and attempt to hold on in an effort to keep his or her face out of the water. This requires a quick reaction on your part. A one- or two-hand block executed quickly may prevent the victim from gaining hold.

One- or Two-Hand Block

The block is designed to prevent the victim from grabbing hold of you. You can make a block by placing the open palm of one hand high on the victim's chest while leaning away and submerging when

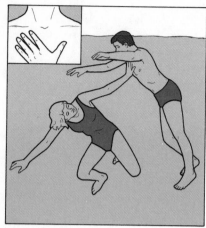

Figure 80
One–Hand Block

the victim attempts to grab you. Remember to keep the arm extended and submerge your head *(Fig. 80)*.

The same result can be obtained by blocking with two hands high on the victim's chest. Keep the arms fully extended while submerging underwater.

After using a block, return quickly to the surface, reassess your position, and approach the victim from behind.

Escapes

If you are grabbed by a victim, there are several options available.

Option 1: Swim to Safety With the Victim Holding On

If the victim is small or buoyant or a short distance to safety, you may choose to swim to safety while the victim holds on. The breaststroke is best if the victim grabs you by the head from the front. The sidestroke or breaststroke could be used if the victim grabs you by the head from behind. Use the sidestroke if you are grabbed by the wrist or upper arm.

Option 2:   Submerge the Victim to Break Contact

The rescuer can choose to break the hold of a victim immediately by pushing or taking him or her underwater. For front and rear head holds, take a breath, tuck the chin, turn your head to either side, raise your shoulders, and use a feetfirst surface dive to take the victim underwater. For a wrist or upper arm hold, reach across with your free hand, place it on the victim's shoulder, and press the victim under water while pulling your hand free. Once underwater, the victim should let go. Once free, return to the surface away from the victim and reassess the situation. Swim to the rear of the victim and use any appropriate tow or carry to take the victim to safety.

Option 3: Escape and Rescue

The third option consists of using one of the following escapes:

- **Front Head–Hold Escape:** As soon as you are grabbed, take a quick breath, tuck your chin, and submerge with the victim *(Fig. 81)*. Turn your head to either side and raise your shoulders to protect your throat. On the way down, bring your hands to the victim's elbows or the undersides of the upper arms, and push vigorously up and away from you *(Fig. 82)*. Keep the chin tucked, your arm fully extended, and your shoulders raised until you get free. Quickly swim on your back or side out of reach. After surfacing, swim around behind the victim, use a rear approach and any appropriate tow or carry to complete the rescue.

Figure 81
Front Head–Hold Escape:
Submerge

Figure 82
Push Up and Away

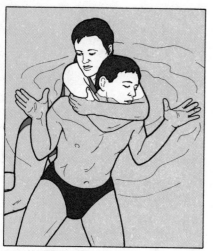

Figure 83
Rear Head–Hold Escape

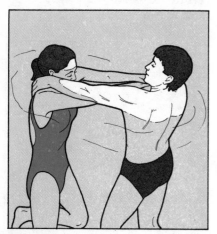

Figure 84
Push Down on Victim's Shoulder

Figure 85
Grab Your Other Hand

- **Rear Head–Hold Escape:** If the victim grabs you from behind, take a quick breath, tuck your chin down, turn your head to either side, and raise your shoulders to protect your throat. Submerge, taking the victim with you. Bring your hands up to the elbows or to the underside of the victim's arms just above the elbows *(Fig. 83)*. Push upward forcefully and twist your head and shoulders until you escape. When the victim releases his or her grasp, swim up and out of reach. Surface and swim behind the victim. Use a rear approach and any appropriate tow or carry to complete the rescue.

- **Wrist–Grip Escape:** If a victim grabs your arm or wrist, quickly submerge the victim by reaching across with your free hand and pushing down on the victim's shoulder while kicking upward for better leverage *(Fig. 84)*. Pull your hand free. You may also reach down with your free hand, grab your other hand, and jerk upward *(Fig. 85)*. Stroke backward quickly with your arms and legs to escape the victim's reach. Swim around behind the victim, use a rear approach, and use any appropriate tow or carry to complete the rescue. Use a scissors, breaststroke, or rotary kick.

Multiple Near-Drowning Maneuver

Occasionally, near-drownings occur that involve two or more people. Often, victims of multiple near-drowning will clutch each other in their panic. A multiple near-drowning should be handled by several lifeguards. This situation calls for the development and use of an emergency action plan designed to bring two or more lifeguards to the accident scene. A one-to-one ratio of lifeguards to victims is best for safety and speed. Should a multiple near-drowning occur at an outdoor facility where water visibility is poor, at least one or more lifeguards should check the bottom for possible submerged victims while the rescue of those on the surface proceeds. A thorough search should be made by several lifeguards as soon as the known victims are provided with emergency care.

If you are the only lifeguard available to handle a multiple near-drowning and you are within a short distance to safety, you should push or tow the victims clutching each other to safety, using a double armpit tow on one of the victims. If the victims are submerged too deep to push or pull to safety, swim to the rear of the victim who has attained the top position. Move your hands quickly to the armpits of that victim while placing one or both feet on the upper chest of the other victim *(Fig. 86)*. Press down and away with the feet (don't kick) while pulling on the armpits of the victim who is in the top position until the two victims are separated. After towing or carrying the first victim to safety, return to assist the other victim. If another rescuer is available, a second rescuer should help the other victim.

Figure 86
Place Feet on Shoulders

Rescue Breathing in the Water

If the victim is not breathing when contacted in deep water, rescue breathing should be started as soon as possible. Rescue breathing can be initiated in deep water using a rescue tube, rescue buoy, rescue board, or if the victim is wearing a water-ski belt, personal flotation device (PFD), or a buoyancy compensating device (BCD).

Deep water rescue breathing without flotation equipment is extremely difficult. A well-conditioned lifeguard helping a small victim may be able to open the airway and give two full breaths. However, sustained rescue breathing may not be possible and could delay getting the victim to safety. In diving pools, the lifeguard's use of swim fins while supporting the victim may make rescue breathing possible if no other flotation is available.

Figure 87
Rescue Breathing: Deep Water

Deep Water Rescue Breathing (Pool or Dockside)

If the victim cannot be removed from the water or brought to shallow water, take the victim to the pool's edge and grab the side of the pool with one hand. Call for help. Pull the victim in close to the side of the pool or deck, place both your feet on the wall or support and position the victim between you and the wall. Support the victim on one of your knees. Reach your right arm between the victim's right arm and side, or your left arm between the victim's left arm and side. Slide your arm under the victim's upper back and grasp the side of the pool or deck **(Fig. 87)**. Place your other hand on the victim's forehead, open the airway, and check for breathing. If victim is not breathing, pinch the nostrils between your index finger and thumb, tilt the head, and give two full breaths. Check for pulse. If there is a pulse but the victim is still not breathing, continue rescue breathing. If there is no pulse, remove the victim from the water as soon as you can and begin CPR.

Shallow Water Rescue Breathing (Pool or Open Water)

Bring the victim into shallow water and position on the back, so that his or her head is positioned near one of your arms. Call for help. Slide your right hand between the victim's right arm and side, and under his or her upper back, keeping your palm turned up to provide support. Place your left hand on the victim's forehead, open the airway, check for breathing. If the victim is not breathing, pinch the nose and give two full breaths. Check for pulse. If there is a pulse, but the victim is still not breathing, continue rescue breathing. If there is no pulse, remove the victim from the water as soon as you can and begin CPR.

Spinal Injury Management

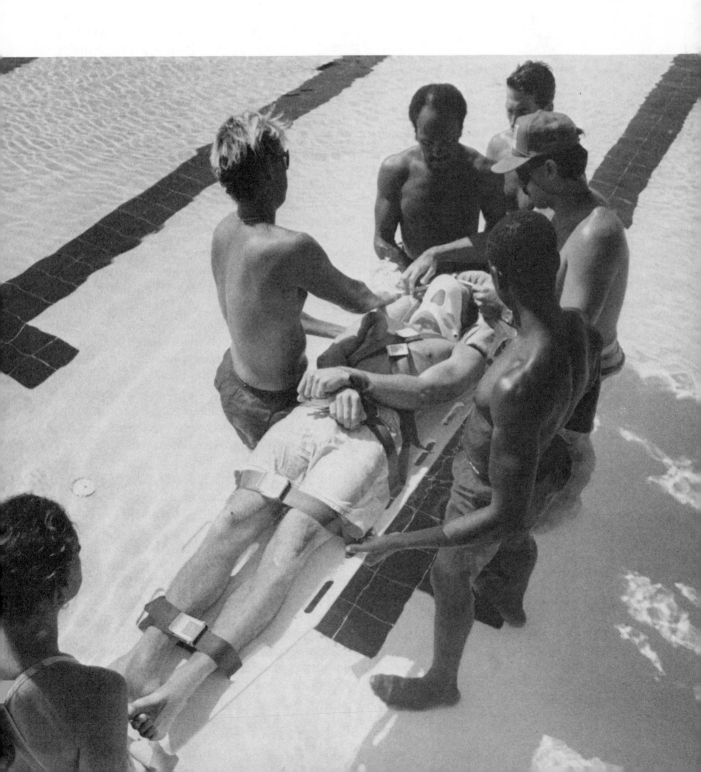

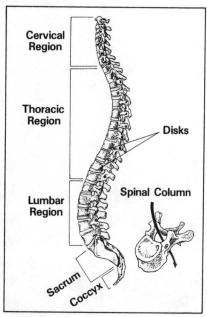

Figure 88
Anatomy of Spine

This section provides information that will help lifeguards recognize a victim with a suspected spinal injury and handle the victim in such a way as to prevent any further injury. Although this section deals with spinal injuries in the water, lifeguards should be trained to handle a victim on the deck or beach as well.

Sports-related injuries comprised 14.2 percent of all spinal cord traumas in 1986.* Sixty-six percent of these sports-related spinal cord injuries were caused by diving. Of these diving injuries, approximately 95 percent occurred in shallow water (5 feet or less).

Rarely does a spinal injury occur from supervised diving or diving off boards into deep water. Spinal injuries that happen in pools most often happen at the shallow end of the pool, in a corner of the pool, or where the bottom drops off into deeper water. At open water facilities, such as lakes or rivers, spinal injuries can occur in areas where water levels vary due to tides or currents, or in areas where there are underwater hazards, such as rocks or tree stumps.

The following section deals with the immediate management of spinal cord trauma for a victim in the water. Appropriate turns to right a prone victim, providing in-line stabilization of the spine, cervical collar placement, proper boarding procedures, and removal from the water are covered.

Anatomy and Function of the Spine

A lifeguard must have a basic understanding of the anatomy and function of the spine in order to provide appropriate immediate care to a victim with a suspected back or neck injury. Most diving-related injuries result in damage to the cervical (neck) region.

The spine is a strong, flexible column that supports the head and the trunk and encloses and provides protection to the spinal cord. The spine consists of small bones (vertebrae) separated from each other by cushions of cartilage called intervertebral disks *(Fig. 88)*. This cartilage acts as a shock absorber when a person is walking, running, or jumping. A vertebra is a circle of bone. The spinal cord runs through the hollow part of the circle. Nerve branches extend to various parts of the body through openings on the sides of the vertebrae.

The spine is divided into five regions: the cervical or neck region, the thoracic or mid-back region, the lumbar or lower back region, the sacrum, and the coccyx, the small triangular bone at the lower end of the spinal column. Injuries to the spinal column include fractures and dislocations of the vertebrae, sprained ligaments, and compression or displacement of the intervertebral disks. Any of these situations can sever or compress the spinal cord resulting in temporary or permanent paralysis or death.

---

* *Spinal Cord Injury: The Facts and Figures*, A Spinal Cord Injury Data Base at the University of Alabama in Birmingham, 1986.

Assessing Spinal Injuries
In trying to determine whether the spinal cord has been injured, you must take into consideration the cause of injury. The following is a general list of situations that may indicate a spinal cord injury:
- Any fall from a height greater than the victim's height
- Any person found unconscious for unknown reasons
- Any significant head trauma
- All diving accidents

Signs and Symptoms of Spinal Injury
The following signs and symptoms may be present:
- Pain at the fracture site
- Loss of movement in the extremities or below the fracture site
- Loss of sensation or tingling in the extremities
- Disorientation
- Back or neck deformity
- Visible bruising over an area of the spinal column
- Impaired breathing
- Head injury
- Fluid or blood in ears

Principles for Handling a Victim of Suspected Spinal Injury

Lifeguards do not have the formal training or the equipment necessary to make an accurate diagnosis of a spinal injury. Therefore, all suspected spinal injuries should be considered fractures and treated accordingly.

The following factors may influence the lifeguard's actions:
- The victim's condition—presence or absence of respiration or pulse
- The lifeguard's size in relation to the victim
- The location of the victim—shallow water, deep water, or on the bottom
- The availability of assistance—additional lifeguards; EMS, police, or fire department personnel; bystanders
- The temperature of the water and/or air

As with any other emergency, an action plan for this type of injury must be established and then rehearsed periodically. Because of the great potential for further injury and risk to the victim, additional precautions must be taken when caring for the victim of spinal injury.

Proper management of the airway must be maintained at all times. Depending on the degree of the injury to the spinal column, the victim may not be breathing or may be experiencing breathing difficulty. If the injury is in the cervical region, there may be paralysis of the chest muscles. Talk to the victim. If the victim can speak, the victim is breathing. In all other cases, the "look, listen,

51

and feel for breathing" steps must be followed, and resuscitation should be started immediately, when necessary. Care must be taken not to move the head forward, backward, or sideways. The modified jaw thrust, therefore, should be used to open the airway and perform rescue breathing for a nonbreathing victim with a suspected spinal injury. In the water, this procedure is best accomplished with a second rescuer. While the first rescuer continues to stabilize the head and neck, the second rescuer performs the modified jaw thrust.

The modified jaw thrust is a method of opening the airway that minimizes movement of the victim's head and neck. From a position at an angle behind the victim's head, the rescuer places his or her hands on both sides of the victim's head and applies pressure to the angles of the lower jaw with the fingers to lift the jaw upwards *(Fig. 89)*. At the same time, the palms of the rescuer's hands keep the victim's head from moving backwards. Detailed steps for learning the modified jaw thrust technique for rescue breathing are taught in the American Red Cross CPR: Basic Life Support for the Professional Rescuer course.

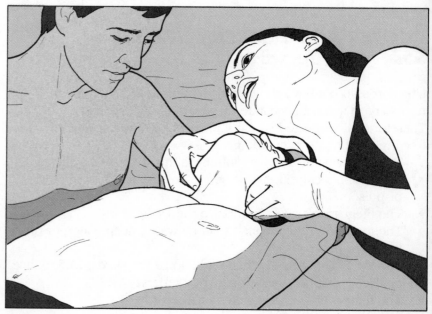

Figure 89
Modified Jaw Thrust

During the rescue procedures, management of the victim can be improved if additional assistance is available. In facilities that use a minimum number of lifeguards, rescuers may have no formal training. To reduce the possibility of this happening and to increase the number of trained people who may be available, these first aid procedures may be included as part of the in-service training program. There should also be education demonstrations and seminars conducted in cooperation with local EMS personnel.

General Rescue Procedures

As previously stated, all suspected spinal injuries should be considered fractures and treated accordingly. The rescue technique used may vary, depending on the situation. The technique selected will depend on the lifeguard's ability to perform it with accuracy and competence.

Regardless of which technique is used, the following principles remain the same:

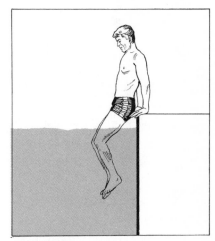

Figure 90
Ease Into Water

- *Activate your facility's emergency action plan.* Other staff will then know there is an emergency, notify EMS, and be ready to assist you.
- *Approach the victim carefully.* Do not jump or dive into a position near the victim. The lifeguard should ease gently into the water *(Fig. 90)*. This reduces the possibility of causing any additional movement of the victim.
- *Reduce or prevent any movement of the victim's spine.* The victim's head, neck, and back must be immobilized. This immobilization technique, called in-line stabilization, prevents movement and is initially done by the use of the lifeguard's hands, arms, or body, depending on which technique is used *(Fig. 91)*.

Figure 91
In–Line Stabilization

- *Move the victim to the surface of the water.* A submerged victim must be brought carefully to the surface before first aid can begin.
- *Rotate the victim to a horizontal position.* The victim's face must be kept out of the water to allow the victim to breathe.

- ***Move the victim to shallow water, if possible.***
  Immobilization of the victim, proper application of a
  backboard, and removal of the victim from the water are more
  easily performed in shallow water. If shallow water is not
  available in all parts of the facility (e.g., victim is in a separate
  diving pool), procedures to provide additional support to the
  lifeguard and the victim must be established and rehearsed. Use
  of swim fins is very helpful for maintaining a victim afloat in
  deep water.
- ***Check for breathing.*** Use a second rescuer to open the
  victim's airway, using the modified jaw thrust. If the victim is not
  breathing, rescue breathing must be started as soon as possible.
  If the victim is breathing, the second rescuer must monitor the
  victim's breathing.
- ***Position the backboard under the victim.*** It is important
  to position the backboard without any unnecessary movement
  of the victim *(Fig. 92)*.

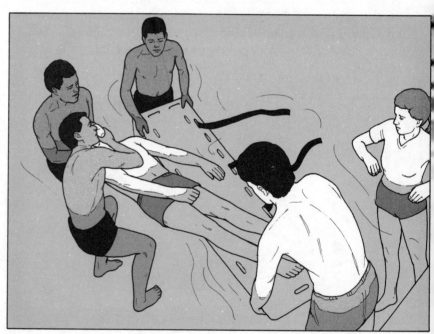

Figure 92
Position Backboard

- **Secure the victim to the backboard.** Strapping is an additional precaution to secure the victim to the board and prevent additional injury to the spine *(Fig. 93)*. Use a rigid cervical collar, a blanket or towel roll, and multiple straps or cravats.

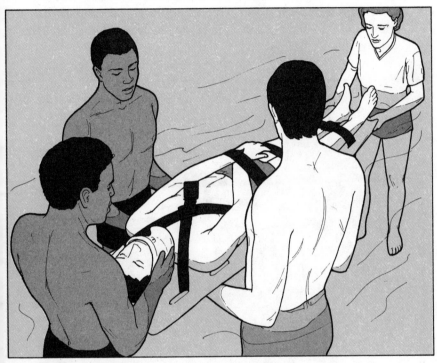

Figure 93
Secure Victim to Board

- **Remove the victim from the water.** If it is necessary to remove the victim from the water prior to the arrival of emergency medical personnel, the backboard should be kept in a horizontal position **(Fig. 94)**. Once on the deck, the victim should be given first aid for shock. The victim's breathing and circulation must be monitored until EMS personnel arrive.
- **Keep the victim warm.** Hypothermia is a serious threat in spinal cord injury because the body's temperature regulation system may be damaged.

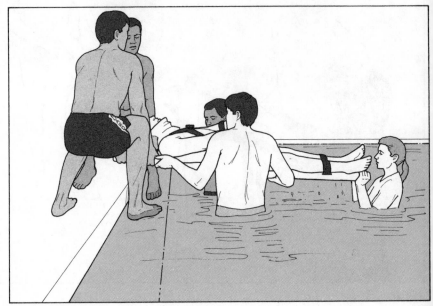

Figure 94
Remove Victim From Water

Specific Rescue Techniques

Several rescue techniques are presented in this chapter. They may be adapted to different situations. Lifeguards should be thoroughly familiar with each technique and should be able to decide which one to use in a particular situation. Some of the steps in a technique may need to be performed simultaneously.

The following points must be considered when choosing a technique:
- The buoyancy of the victim
- The buoyancy of the lifeguard
- The victim's size
- The lifeguard's size
- The power of the lifeguard's leg stroke
- The lifeguard's breath-holding capability
- Position of the victim—faceup or facedown

- Location of the victim—deep or shallow water, on or near the surface or underwater
- Wind and water conditions

Techniques for Stabilizing Suspected Spinal Injuries (Shallow Water)

Several rescue techniques can be used for limiting movement or immobilizing suspected spinal injuries:
- Hip and shoulder support (limits movement but does not actually immobilize)
- Head splint
- Head/chin support

Hip and Shoulder Support
If the victim is faceup and no help is immediately available to assist in boarding (placing the victim on a backboard), support the victim at the hips and shoulders, keeping the face clear of the water for breathing. This technique is for calm, shallow water only.
- Stand facing the victim's side, and lower yourself to chest depth.
- Slide one arm under the shoulders and the other under the hip bones and support the victim *(Fig. 95)*.

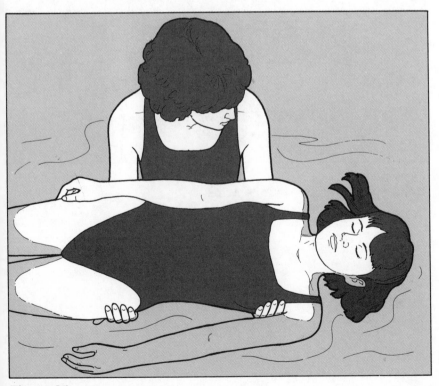

Figure 95
Hip and Shoulder Support

- Do not lift the victim, but maintain the victim in a horizontal position in the water until help arrives.
- Comfort and reassure the victim.

Head Splint

Victims who are facedown in the water must be turned faceup immediately to allow them to breathe. This technique for immobilizing the head and neck can be used in calm or choppy water, and deep or shallow water.

- Stand facing the victim's side.
- Gently float the victim's arms up alongside the head, parallel to the surface. Do this by grasping the victim's arms midway between the shoulder and elbow *(Fig. 96)*.

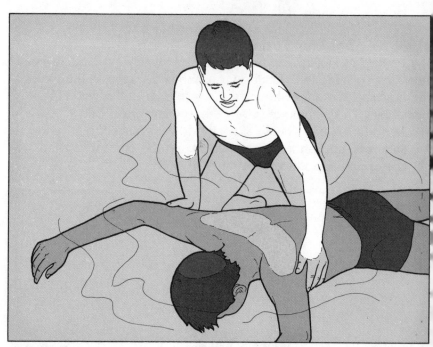

Figure 96
Head Splint: Grasp Victim's Arms

- With your right hand, grasp the victim's right arm. With your left hand, grasp victim's left arm. Position the arms so they are extended against the victim's head *(Fig. 97)*.

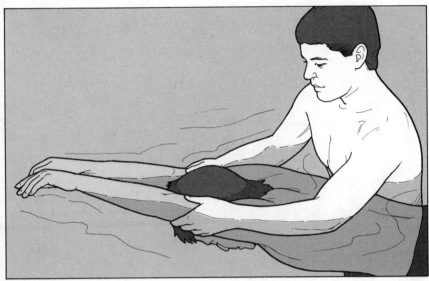

Figure 97
Head Splint: Position Arms Against Victim's Head

- When the victim's arms are extended over the head and in line with the body, apply pressure to the arms to splint the head. Generally, your hands will be approximately at the victim's ears. This technique for stabilizing the head provides in-line stabilization.
- Lower your body to chest depth in the water and start to move the victim slowly forward to a horizontal position, gliding the victim's body to the surface. This reduces body twist when the turn is made.
- Once the victim is horizontal in the water, continue moving and rotate the victim toward you by pushing the arm closer to you underwater while pulling the victim's other arm across the surface to turn the victim faceup *(Fig. 98)*. As you do this, lower your shoulders in the water.

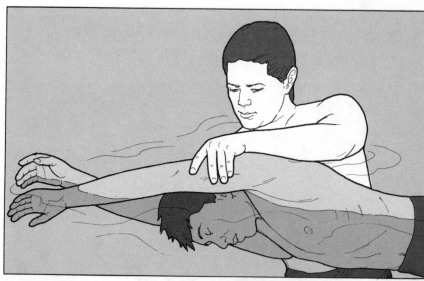

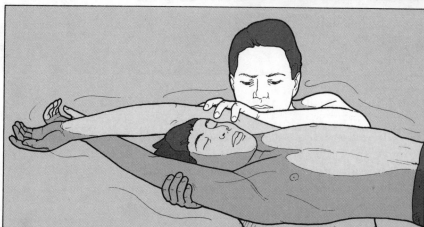

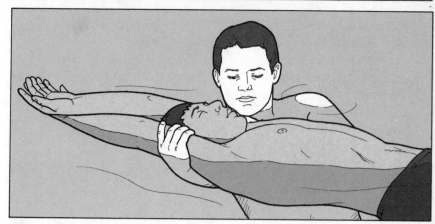

Figure 98
Head Splint: Rotate Victim Faceup

- Rest the victim's head in the crook of your arm, but not **on** your arm.
- Maintain the victim in a horizontal position in the water until help arrives.

Head/Chin Support

A third technique for immobilizing the spine is called head/chin support. This technique can be used in any type or condition of water and on both faceup and facedown victims.

- Approach from either side of the victim. You may have to move the victim's arm that is nearer you so that the victim's shoulder and arm will be against your chest.
- Lower your body until your shoulders are at water level.
- Place your forearms along the length of the victim's breastbone and spine. One hand is used to support the victim's chin. The thumb of that hand is on one side of the victim's chin and the fingers are on the other side *(Fig. 99)*. Do not apply pressure yet.

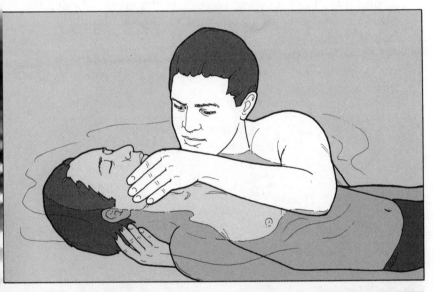

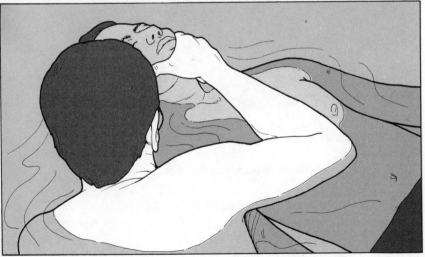

Figure 99
Head/Chin: Hand Position

Figure 100
Head/Chin: Rotate Victim
Faceup

- At the same time, your other hand supports the victim's head at the base of the skull by using your thumb on one side of the head and your fingers on the other side. Do not apply pressure yet.
- Lock both of your wrists and squeeze your forearms together, clamping the victim's chest and back between them. Apply gentle pressure to the chin and the base of the skull. You are now providing in-line stabilization.
- Glide the victim forward to a horizontal position.
- If the victim is facedown, you will need to turn the victim faceup. To turn victim faceup, rotate the victim toward you. Submerge, carefully go under the victim as you turn the victim faceup, and surface on the other side *(Fig. 100)*. This movement must be done slowly to reduce any twisting of the victim's body.
- Maintain the victim in a horizontal position in the water until help arrives.
- When sufficient help arrives, a second rescuer assists in providing in-line stabilization by placing both hands alongside the victim's head *(Fig. 101)*.

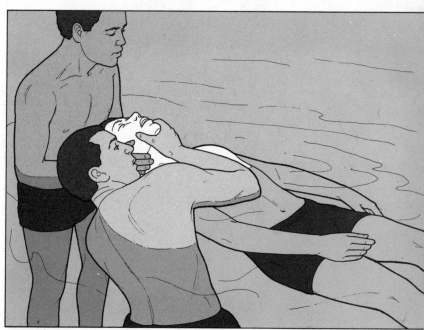

Figure 101
Head/Chin: In–Line Stabilization by Second Rescuer

The head/chin support technique can also be used with a victim who is submerged and who may be lying on his or her front, back, or side. Victims with spinal injuries are rarely found on the bottom in deep water. However, if you do encounter a victim in this position, you should perform the steps as described in this section and bring the victim to the surface at a 45-degree angle. Using this

echnique, you can then move the victim to shallow water. Always
e sure to exercise extreme caution to prevent any movement of
he victim's head or neck.

Boarding Procedures

After stabilizing the victim's head and neck by using any of the
previously described techniques, place a backboard under the
victim.

- The initial rescuer provides direction to the assistants, directing
  them to do the following:
  —Bring the backboard into the water and approach the victim
    from the side.
  —Place the backboard diagonally under the victim from the side,
    with the foot end of the board going down in the water first
    (Fig. 102).

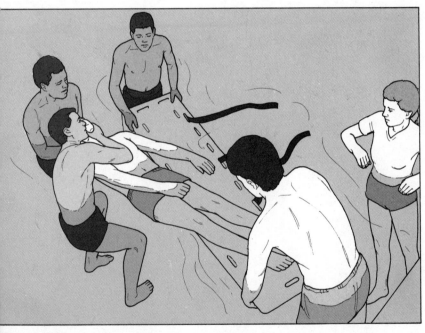

Figure 102
Position the Backboard

—Hold the board down under the water so it doesn't bump
    against the victim, and slide it under the victim and position it
    lengthwise along the victim's spine. Make sure the board is
    beyond the victim's head near the rescuer maintaining in-line
    stabilization.
—Allow the board to rise under the victim. At least one rescuer
    should be along each side of the board, and one at the victim's
    feet.
- The rescuer stabilizing the victim's head and neck should slowly
  and carefully withdraw his or her arms as the board is raised into
  place against the victim.

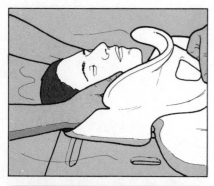

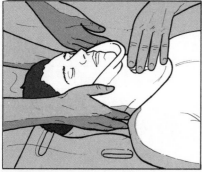

Figure 103
Place Cervical Collar

- After the board is in place, a rigid cervical collar must be applied. While a second rescuer maintains in-line stabilization, the first rescuer carefully applies an appropriate-sized rigid cervical collar. The cervical collar should fit securely with the chin in the proper resting position and with the head maintained in the neutral position by the collar *(Fig. 103)*.
- After the cervical collar is in place, secure the victim to the backboard using straps or cravats.
  —Begin by securing the victim's shoulders by criss-crossing the chest and securing at the sides *(Fig. 104)*. The straps should be snug, but not so tight as to restrict movement of the chest during normal breathing.
  —Secure the strap across the hip bones.

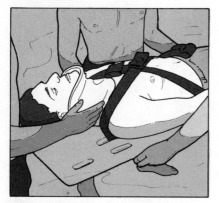

Figure 104
Secure Victim's Shoulders

–Secure the hands alongside or in front of the victim *(Fig. 105)*.

–Secure the thighs and shins to the backboard *(Fig. 106)*. If additional support is needed, put a figure-8 tie on the ankles so that the feet do not move.

–Secure the head. Before securing the head to the board, it may be necessary to place padding, such as a folded towel, under the victim's head *(Fig. 107)*. The amount of padding needed will be evident from the space between the board and the head while in-line stabilization is maintained. Normally, approximately one inch of padding is all that is needed to keep the head in a neutral position and provide comfort for the victim.

–Continue to secure the head by placing a towel or blanket roll in a horseshoe configuration around the head and neck of the victim *(Fig. 108)*.

Figure 105
Secure Victim's Hands

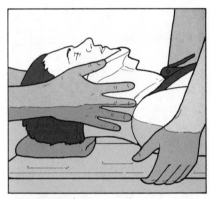

Figure 107
Padding Under Head

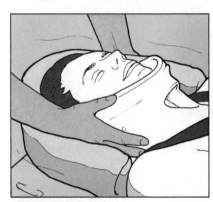

Figure 108
Secure Head With Blanket or Towel

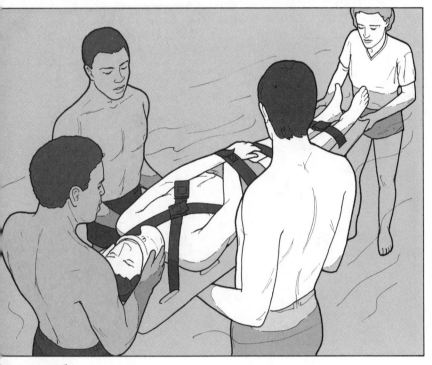

Figure 106
Secure Thighs and Shins

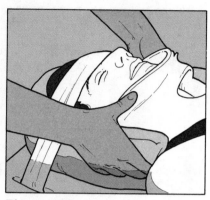

Figure 109
Secure Forehead

- Secure the forehead with whatever material your facility uses *(Fig. 109)*. This could include velcro straps, cravats, cling, or other conforming material. Instead of the towel rolls, some E. systems provide head immobilizing kits that secure the head t the board. Your local facility must make the decision regardin, what to use.

Note: Alternate methods of strapping may be used provided the technique meets the objectives for immobilization of the spine.

Removal From Water
- Once the victim is secured to the board, remove the victim fr the water. The rescuer at the head should direct the removal.
- If in a pool, move the victim to the side of the pool.
- Position the board perpendicular to the side of the pool. The board should be kept as horizontal as possible while it is bein; removed.
- Remove the board headfirst *(Fig. 110)*. You may have to tip the board at the head to break the initial suction holding it in t water.

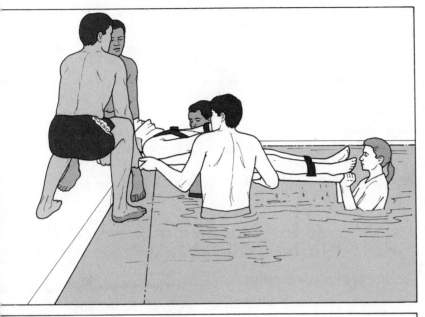

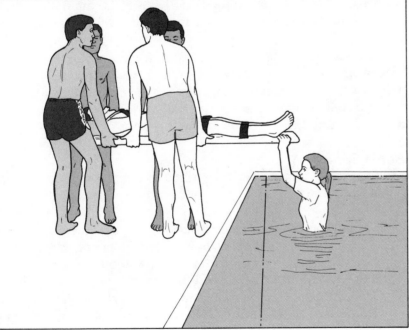

Figure 110
Remove Board

- If EMS personnel have arrived, they will be available to help in the removal of the victim. Depending on the location in which you live, EMS personnel may or may not go in the water.
- Two people should be on the deck or dock to help lift and slide the board onto the pool deck. The person at the victim's head can either move to the pool deck or help at the sides, depending on how many persons are available to help.
- The board and victim are removed slowly and carefully.
- Once the victim is removed from the water, give first aid for shock.
- Continue to monitor the victim's consciousness and breathing.

Techniques for Stabilizing Suspected Spinal Injuries (Deep Water)

Fortunately, it is rare for a person to suffer a deep water spinal injury. Because lifeguards cannot evaluate a spinal fracture, all head, neck, or back injuries must be cared for as possible spinal injuries. If the injury occurs in deep water, move the victim to shallow water, if possible.

Lifeguards at diving pools with no shallow water access should have swim fins available at their chair. Fins will allow the lifeguard to move easily and keep the victim of a suspected spinal fracture on the surface until additional help arrives. At least five additional rescuers are necessary for deep water support.

Head Splint
- Keep the victim afloat as described in the previous section on shallow water support. The initial rescuer maintains the head splint using the victim's arms.
- If a rescuer cannot swim to shallow water with the victim, the initial rescuer should maintain the head splint and swim to the edge of the pool or a ladder area where another rescuer can help support the initial rescuer and the victim.
- Once additional rescuers are available, one should hold the victim's feet at the surface while one or two other rescuers place a backboard under the victim.
- Have another rescuer lie or kneel on the deck and provide in-line stabilization.
- As the board is moved upward, the initial rescuer releases the victim's arms.
- The victim's arms are gently positioned at his or her sides.
- The placement of the cervical collar, strapping, and removal from the water now continue.

Head/Chin Support

- Use the head/chin support technique to turn the victim faceup, if necessary, so the victim can breathe.
- Tread water with swim fins on or swim in wide circles with the victim until additional help is available. If a platform is available, use it.
- Swim with the victim to the closest corner or pool ladder until a second rescuer can help support the initial rescuer. If using a pool ladder, place your foot on one of the steps for temporary support.
- Once additional rescuers are available, one should hold the victim's feet at the surface while one or two other rescuers place a backboard under the victim.
- Have another rescuer lie or kneel on the deck and provide in-line stabilization.
- As the backboard is moved upwards, the initial rescuer withdraws his or her arms.
- The placement of the cervical collar, strapping, and removal from the water now continue.

5 Special Situations

Hypothermia

Lifeguards need to know about exposure to cold temperatures and the potential for hypothermia. This section deals with the causes and effects of exposure to cold temperatures, the signs and symptoms of hypothermia, and first aid for hypothermia victims. Methods of preventing hypothermia and treatment of victims of hypothermia are also presented.

Hypothermia refers to a low body temperature, specifically a low body-core temperature (temperature of the vital organs). Hypothermia occurs when cold or cool temperatures cause the body to lose heat faster than it can be produced, and the body-core temperature falls below normal.

Factors that influence the onset and progression of hypothermia are—

- Air and water temperatures.
- Wind speed.
- Length of exposure.
- Amount and type of clothing worn.
- The individual's age, body size, and body build.
- The mental and physical condition of the individual.
- Acclimatization to cold-water exposure.

The body loses heat through the following four processes:

- Conduction—Heat lost through body contact with a cold object, such as water or the ground
- Convection—Heat lost through air or water movement around the body
- Radiation—Heat lost to still air that surrounds the body, such as cold air with no wind
- Evaporation—Heat lost through water evaporating on the skin, such as perspiration

Signs and Signals

When the body temperature begins to drop, the body reacts to correct the heat loss. The body reduces the flow of blood to the extremities in an attempt to prevent further heat loss. Shivering—usually a series of rapid, involuntary muscle contractions—is an example of the body's efforts to increase heat production. The following list identifies the body's reactions to decreases in body-core temperature.

Degree of Hypothermia	Description
Mild	The victim is conscious and alert but breathing deeply. There is vigorous, uncontrollable shivering. The ability to perform simple tasks is impaired.
Moderate	The victim is conscious but mental faculties and speech are impaired. The voice is lowered. There is loss of coordination. The victim performs simple tasks with much difficulty. Shivering lessens.
Severe	The victim may be unconscious. Mental faculties are severely impaired. Shivering is replaced by muscle rigidity (stiffness). The victim's skin may become cyanotic (bluish). Respiration and pulse become slower. The victim is totally unable to perform simple tasks.
Very Severe	The victim is usually unconscious. This stage may be preceded by irrationality. Respiration and pulse continue to slow. Rigidity (stiffness) persists. Abnormal cardiac and respiratory rhythms may occur.
Critical	The victim is unconscious and reflexes are nonfunctioning. Respiration is barely detectable. There is severe cardiac irregularity leading to ventricular fibrillation, cardiac arrest, and death.

Caring for Hypothermia
Mild to Moderate Hypothermia

Swimmers under the age of 12 are especially vulnerable to cold water. Be alert to individuals showing the first signs of hypothermia, such as bluish lips or shivering. These swimmers should be moved to a warm area. If they are not already indoors, move them indoors. Keep them in an area where there is little air movement, such as an office or first aid room. Cover them with a blanket until the hypothermia symptoms disappear. You may give warm liquids. Do not give alcoholic beverages or those containing caffeine.

Severe to Critical Hypothermia

Swimmers exhibiting the signs and symptoms for severe to critical hypothermia should be handled as carefully as victims of spinal injuries and kept in a horizontal position. Call EMS immediately. Do not allow these victims to move around after being removed from the water. Do not rub or massage the victim's extremities. Any form of exercise will increase the flow of cold blood from the extremities back to the body core, which will increase the chances for "afterdrop." Afterdrop is the further decrease of an already lowered body-core temperature. It is caused by cold, metabolically imbalanced blood being sent from the extremities of the body back to the core. The effect of this blood on highly sensitive heart tissue can lead to cardiac irregularities, such as ventricular fibrillation or cardiac arrest. Afterdrop can be fatal, especially to those swimmers whose core temperature is 90.3°F or below.

Prevention and Treatment

The following are the first aid procedures for handling swimmers who are victims of hypothermia:

- *In the case of severe to critical hypothermia, call EMS immediately.*
- *Maintain an open airway for the victim, if necessary.* Begin rescue breathing or CPR, if necessary. Before starting CPR, you may need to check the victim's pulse for up to one minute because of the slower pulse rate in hypothermia.
- *Prevent further heat loss.* Allow the body temperature to return to normal gradually. Provide warm, dry clothing. Wrap the victim in blankets, dry towels, several layers of clothing, or all of these items. Avoid direct contact with hot objects or high temperatures to warm the victim. If available, hot water bottles, heating pads, or chemical heat packs can be used, but they should be wrapped in a towel or blanket to prevent burning the victim. These items are used to rewarm only the trunk, groin, neck, and head, since these areas of the body have the highest rates of heat loss. These areas, however, also transfer warmth to the body core faster than the extremities. Do not apply warming items such as heating pads to the extremities. This warmth will dilate the blood vessels in the extremities, allowing cold blood to return more rapidly to the body core.

Give warm liquids, such as broth, if the victim is conscious and able to swallow. Do not give liquids to an unconscious victim.

Do not allow the victim to smoke. Nicotine reduces circulation to the skin, which increases the risk of cold injury.

- *Do not give the victim any alcoholic beverages or any beverages containing caffeine.* Alcohol and caffeine both cause increased urination, which can interfere with the body's defenses against hypothermia. Alcohol prevents the normal shivering response and therefore decreases heat production.
- *Any victim of severe to critical hypothermia must receive immediate medical care.*

Heat Emergencies

These problems often occur when swimmers play too long and hard or stay too long in the sun. People do not always realize how the sun can affect them.

Because sunlight reflects off shiny surfaces such as bodies of water, being around water can increase your exposure. Sunburn can occur on overcast days as well as on sunny days. When swimmers are in the sun, they should wear a water-resistant sunscreen lotion, which blocks some sun rays, or a sunblock lotion, which provides maximum protection. Sunglasses and a hat provide added protection.

The following information tells how to recognize heat stroke, heat exhaustion, and heat cramps, and what to do for victims of these conditions.

Heat Stroke
Signs and Symptoms
- Hot, red skin
- Very high body temperature
- Shock or unconsciousness

What to Do
- Treat heat stroke as a life-threatening emergency, and call EMS.
- Get the victim into the coolest place available.
- Cool the victim by immersing in a cool bath or wrapping in wet sheets and fanning.
- Care for shock by lying the victim down and elevating the feet.
- Give nothing by mouth.

Heat Exhaustion
Signs and Symptoms
- Cool, pale, moist skin
- Rapid, weak pulse
- Weakness/dizziness
- Nausea/vomiting

What to Do
- Treat heat exhaustion as an emergency, and call EMS.
- Get the victim into the coolest place available.
- Place the victim on the back with the feet elevated.
- Cool victim by applying wet sheets or towels to the body and b fanning.
- Give ½ .glass of water to drink every 15 minutes if the victim is fully conscious and can tolerate it.

Heat Cramps
Signs and Symptoms
Muscular pains and spasms, usually in the legs or abdomen

What to Do
- Get the victim into the coolest place available.
- Give ½ glass of water to drink every 15 minutes for an hour.

Prevention
- Seek protection from the sun and extreme heat.
- Replace fluids by drinking water, sports drinks, or fruit juices.

Seizures

Overview
The normal functions of the brain can be disturbed by a variety of conditions, such as injury, infection, or disease. When this occurs, the electrical activity of the brain can become irregular. This irregular activity can cause sudden, uncontrolled muscle contractions known as seizures.

Types of Seizures
There are several types of seizures, ranging from those characterized by brief loss of consciousness without muscular contractions (petit mal), to those with loss of consciousness and violent muscular contractions (grand mal).

Signs and Symptoms of Seizures
In the same way that types of seizures differ, so do the signs and symptoms. Someone experiencing a petit mal seizure may suddenly stare off into space for a few seconds and then return to full alertness without experiencing any muscular contractions. Someone experiencing a grand mal seizure will usually have the following signs and symptoms:

- An aura. This is a peculiar sensation that may precede a seizure. It usually lasts a few seconds and may consist of visual or auditory hallucinations, a painful sensation, a peculiar taste in the mouth, awareness of a smell, or a sensation warning the victim to move to safety.
- Rigidity of the body, which may be preceded by a high-pitched cry.
- Loss of consciousness.
- Uncontrolled muscular movement. During this phase, the victim may lose bladder and bowel control. The victim may salivate, hold his or her breath, and the heart rate will increase.
- Once the seizure has subsided, the victim will enter a state of drowsiness and confusion, gradually regain consciousness, and complain of a headache.

First Aid for Seizures

First aid care for an individual experiencing a seizure includes the following:
- Prevent the victim from being injured. Clear the area of any hard or sharp objects and loosen tight clothing.
- Do not restrain the victim if he or she is having muscular contractions.
- Do not place anything in the victim's mouth.
- Turn the victim on his or her side if necessary to allow saliva or vomit to drain from the mouth.
- Have someone phone the EMS system.
- Stay with the victim until trained medical professionals arrive. Continue to monitor the victim's breathing. If breathing stops at anytime, begin rescue breathing according to the procedures defined by the American Red Cross.
- Provide an area where the victim can rest and be observed. Be reassuring and supportive. Protect the victim's privacy by removing onlookers.

All individuals who have had a seizure in the water and who have been submerged, regardless of their apparent recovery once out of the water, should receive care from trained medical professionals. In the case of a minor or a mentally incompetent individual, a parent or adult guardian should be informed of the seizure.

An individual who has a seizure while in the water presents additional problems. First, the victim will go under the water quickly, probably without warning or a call for help. Second, the victim will not be able to assist in his or her own rescue. There will not be any resistance to rescue, however, except possibly from convulsive spasms. Third, the victim will probably have an unprotected airway and can breathe in a large amount of water, so special precautions should be taken and medical attention should be sought. Any swimmer who has breathed in large quantities of water, especially fresh water, may develop significant life-threatening medical complications within 30 to 60 minutes. Last, once the victim has been removed from the water, it will be difficult to determine whether abnormalities in the victim's condition are due to a near-drowning or to the after-effects of the seizure.

If a swimmer is suffering a seizure in the water, your first efforts should be to support the victim so that the head and face remain above the water to provide a clear airway. The use of flotation equipment for the victim may be helpful in this situation. The victim should be removed from the pool, taking care to avoid an injury caused by uncontrolled arm and leg movements. EMS should be called.

Once the victim is removed from the pool, the victim's breathing and pulse must be checked. Once you are sure the victim is breathing, the victim should be positioned on his or her side to allow any fluids to drain from the mouth. The victim should now be cared for in the same manner as those having seizures out of the water.

Notes

Notes

Notes

Notes

Notes

Notes

Notes

Notes

Notes

Notes

Notes

Notes